Baby and Beyond

Progression in Play for Babies and Children

Counting

Published 2008 by A&C Black Publishers Limited
38 Soho Square, London W1D 3HB
www.acblack.com

ISBN 978-1-906029-449
Text © Clare Beswick 2008
Series Editor: Sally Featherstone Illustrations © Martha Hardy 2008

A CIP record for this publication is available from the British Library.

Printed in Great Britain by Latimer & Company Limited

This book is produced using paper that is made from wood grown in managed, sustainable forests. It is natural, renewable and recyclable. The logging and manufacturing processes conform to the environmentalregulations of the country of origin.

To see our full range of titles
visit **www.acblack.com**

Contents

Baby and Beyond

A series of books for practitioners working with children from birth to five and beyond

This book gives ideas for introducing and extending role play activities and experiences for babies and young children. Each page spread contains a range of experiences and a selection of ideas for each of the developmental stages of the Early Years Foundation Stage (EYFS). Developmental stages 4, 5 and 6 have been combined over two sections.

Birth - 11 months

Developmental Stage 1

8 - 20 months

Developmental Stage 2

16 - 26 months

Developmental Stage 3

22 - 40 months

Developmental Stage 4 and 5

40 - 60+ months

Developmental Stage 5 and 6

Counting is a fundamental part of everyday experiences and is a skill needed in every part of our lives. Babies and young children begin to develop an understanding of number and counting skills as they make connections and find patterns and order in the objects and experiences they encounter. Play is the perfect medium for discovering and learning about counting.

For very young babies experiences of bringing two objects together in the midline, clapping hands, and discovering fingers and toes are the very first stages in developing an understanding of number. Older babies begin to discover objects that match, starting to develop first sorting skills and then learning about possession - mummy's shoes, baby's shoes - as the first step towards one-to-one correspondence. Young children will enjoy counting together, joining in with simple rhymes and songs and beginning to discover the concept of number, distinguishing between quantities. Older children will enjoy a wide range of games and puzzles and use number and counting in their creative and imaginative play as well as in their use of technology and discovery of their world. Towards the end of the foundation stage children should be confident in their counting skills, counting confidently to ten and more, and back down again to zero. Children will be beginning to count in twos, fives and tens, and be able to use their counting skills in practical situations.

The development of the mathematical language of counting goes hand in hand with the development of counting skill. Babies and young children move from understanding and then using gestures, signs and words for words and phrases, such as all gone, more, again, lots, a few, greater, fewer, hundreds, thousands, millions, as well as the number words, and of course, first/second/third etc.

This book is laid out in progressions across the Early Years Foundation Stage, showing how counting can be developed using everyday activities familiar to all early years practitioners.

The role of the practitioner is crucial, as a facilitator confident in their own numeracy skills. You will be aware of the importance of enabling babies and children to make discoveries, supporting and extending their knowledge, having fun, motivating and providing a wide range of interesting and challenging open-ended activities. Using simple mathematical language and providing commentary will enhance children's play and learning. Singing, music and active play are all critical parts of developing counting skills in babies and young children. The activities in this book are designed to appeal to children using different schemas, and with different learning styles and interests. There should be something to grab the attention of all children, making learning about counting and number easy and enjoyable.

Most importantly, practitioners' greatest challenge and opportunity is to consider every aspect of their time with babies and children and how developing early counting skills can become an integral part of every part of the day, creating real opportunities for children to make choices and use their emerging skills and understanding.

Some other Featherstone Education publications supporting the ideas in this book are: The Little Book of Bricks and Boxes; The Little Book of Role Play; The Little Book of Outdoor Play; The Little book of Prop Boxes for Role Play; The Little Book of Small World Play; What If? role play packs; Inside Out.

all available from www.acblack.com/featherstone

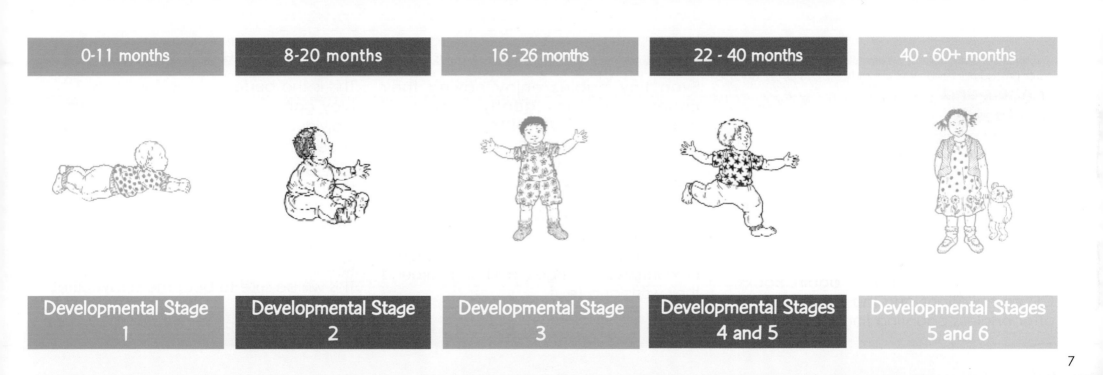

| 0-11 months | 8-20 months | 16 - 26 months | 22 - 40 months | 40 - 60+ months |

| Developmental Stage 1 | Developmental Stage 2 | Developmental Stage 3 | Developmental Stages 4 and 5 | Developmental Stages 5 and 6 |

Fingers and Toes

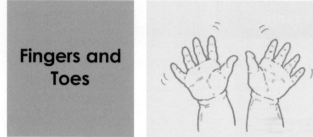

The ultimate, one minute anywhere, anytime resource for counting. Ideal for finger play and number rhymes, for tapping, pointing, clapping and stamping and of course counting to ten and back again. Books, CD compilations and the internet all offer endless counting finger rhymes.

Young babies (0-11 months)

Even tiny babies enjoy having their fingers and toes gently massaged and tickled. Trail different fabrics gently across fingers and toes. By around three months babies press their palms together and enjoy watching and playing with their fingers. By six months they will begin to use a palmar grasp to hold small toys in two hands. Draw their attention to their hands and toes by placing brightly coloured soft bangles and rings around their wrists and feet.

Developmental Stage 1

Babies (8-20 months)

This is the perfect stage for finger play games, and rhymes of all sorts. Try individual sessions with the baby on your knee, and at different times hold them facing you, sideways on your knee, or facing away from you towards another practitioner and baby. This is also a good time for 'One, Two, Three, Go!' games. Build brick towers, say 'One, Two, Three, Go!' – then knock them over together. This will be sure to become a favourite!

Developmental Stage 2

Young children (16-26 months)

Imitating and turn taking are essential parts of the play of children around this age. Try clapping and counting 'One, Two, Three' then lift and swing children gently, with a 'One, Two, Three, wheeee!' or do the same thing when walking with a child between two adults. Make numbers a part of the everyday language as the children imitate simple pretend play, such as picking up or setting out plates cups etc. with 'One, Two, Three'.

Developmental Stage 3

Children (22-40 months)

Children now begin to know some number words but need to move on to matching one object to one count. Make time every day for counting finger rhymes, such as 'Five Fat Peas' or 'One Potato, Two Potato'. Use simple finger puppets, smiley faces or star stickers on each finger. Play, 'Show me three stars', and so on. Count to five or to ten with the older children. Begin to use the language of number, such as 'more,' 'less,' 'lots,' 'a few,' as well as number words.

Developmental Stages 4 & 5

Older children (40-60+ months)

By this stage children should be able to glance at a small group of objects and know that there are say three or five objects. Put a group of three cars on the mat and ask the children to show you the same number of fingers. Talk about how many more to make five cars, how many will there be if two cars drive away. Take off shoes and socks and use fingers and toes for counting to ten, and of course, back again to zero.

Developmental Stages 5 & 6

Drums and Shakers

Real and improvised musical instruments and a lively animated voice are great ways of helping children to feel the steady beat of counting and for older children to match the beat to each count. Drums and shakers are a real motivator for most children, specially those who need something in their hands.

Young babies (0-11 months)

From around six months, babies will love to hold rattles and pass them from hand to hand. Try lots of different rattles and shakers, making lots of different types of sound. Later, babies will enjoy reaching and grasping for toys, and actively exploring objects to hear the sounds they can make. Create treasure baskets of shakers and sound makers, offer choices of sounds makers. Use words, gestures or signs for 'more' and 'all gone'.

Developmental Stage 1

Babies (8-20 months)

Imitate a child's repeated actions, for example, if they bang a pan with a spoon, copy them and then wait to see if they will repeat their action for you to copy again. Use 'Ready Steady Go' and 'One, Two, Three' as cues before shaking a bunch of keys, banging lids together, or striking a chime bar. Be sure to explore the sounds to be made with everyday objects as well as traditional instruments.

Developmental Stage 2

Young children (16-26 months)

At this stage children are often fascinated with putting objects in and then taking them out of containers. Count the shakers together as they go into a tin and then count together as they come out. Use the language of counting - 'more' 'less' 'all gone' 'lots' 'few' as well as number words, as you provide a simple commentary for exploratory play. Listen for and count together everyday sounds, such as dogs barking, clocks chiming and so on.

Developmental Stage 3

Children (22-40 months)

Use a drum or beater to emphasise each count as you count objects or actions together. Play listening games where children listen to and count sounds. Talk about how many beats. Can they make the same number of beats? Try turn taking and copying games with lots of different sounds, such as one bang of a drum, then two rings of a bell and so on. Offer time for children to explore the sounds individually as well with other children.

Developmental Stages 4 & 5

Older children (40-60+ months)

Give five strong beats of the drum or five strikes on a chime bar, as you count back from five to zero, before the children all jump in the air. See if they can play this game, counting the beats silently in their heads. With older children, confident in counting and number play, Try counting back from ten, counting in pairs, two, four, six and so on. Why not make a noisy number line, one drum, two chime bars, three shakers, four bells and so on to ten or twenty?

Developmental Stages 5 & 6

11

Everday Objects

Exploring the familiar and everyday is essential to making sense of the world and establishing early concepts of number and counting. Babies and young children are very focused on the ordinary and their worlds revolve around familiar places and people, so the exploration of this world is and essential foundation of learning.

Young babies (0-11 months)

Create some treasure baskets of everyday objects to explore and count. Choose objects that are interesting to handle, easy to grasp and meaningful to the baby. For younger babies, hang suitable everyday objects from a baby gym frame for patting. Try placing suitable objects such as a glove over the baby's hand for them to pull and tug at. When it is tugged or shaken off, say 'gone', and ask 'again?'.

Developmental Stage 1

Babies (8-20 months)

Collect some pairs of objects - two spoons, two books, two cups, two mittens, two brushes. Put them in a basket and encourage the baby to explore them. When thry find two matching objects, say 'same'. Count with babies as you involve them in everyday routines, such as mealtimes, dressing, washing and so on. Count the bumps the pushchair goes over, the pieces of fruit you put in their bowl, buttons as you fasten them and so on.

Developmental Stage 2

Young children (16-26 months)

Young children love imitating and helping with everyday chores. Count together as you pick up books, tidy away the bricks or toys, collect the cups, throw balls into a box, climb the steps outside. Provide plenty of opportunities for talking about numbers. Look at the pretend play resources in your setting and make sure that there are plenty of duplicate items and sets of objects to encourage comparing, matching, sorting and counting.

Developmental Stage 3

Children (22-40 months)

Provide everyday objects for counting, sorting and matching in the water and sand trays. Use mathematical language such as 'more' 'many' 'lots' 'a few' as you play alongside the children. Encourage children to guess as well as count objects with you. Remember that children at this stage are fascinated by hidden objects, so hide groups of everyday objects in small boxes, bags or containers, then shake, guess how many, empty and count together.

Developmental Stages 4 & 5

Older children (40-60+ months)

Make a treasure basket of everyday objects with numbers, such as rulers, tape measures, calculators, barcodes, mobile phones and so on. Remember to include sets of objects for counting, a big bunch of keys, a purse full of coins, a box of pens. Try a treasure basket of pairs of matching objects, such as two shoes, two bricks, two books, two spoons and so on for matching and counting in twos, or use a Noah's Ark for counting in twos.

Developmental Stages 5 & 6

13

Out and About

Shopping, travelling and walks to the park offer lots of chances for babies and young children to learn about number and counting. Exploring shapes, colours and patterns in the natural world not only presents counting possibilities but enables children to become familiar with and confident in the use of mathematical language.

Young babies (0-11 months)

Talk and sing to babies as you shop, placing items one at a time in a basket, counting as you go. Give a young baby one small item to hold and when it is dropped say 'Gone'. Count kerbs and steps as the pushchair rumbles over them. Explore the feel and texture of objects as you count them. Offer choices and ask, 'more?'. Let children explore the natural world safely, sitting in lots of leaves, counting cones or shells, looking at flowers, nuts, pebbles.

Developmental Stage 1

Babies (8-20 months)

Babies learn by doing, so count the stamps you make together in a puddle, the taps on a railing, the number of times the baby comes to you as you push a swing and so on. Try lots of 'Ready Steady Go,' and 'One, Two, Three, Go,' games rolling a ball, throwing leaves, tssing pebbles in a puddle. To help babies towards one-to-one correspondence, talk about objects and who they belong to, such as mummy's hat, Joe's hat, Jilly's teddy.

Developmental Stage 2

Young children (16-26 months)

Focus on the important numbers for the child - two candles on a birthday cake, the number of sandwiches on a plate, their cars. Count together to three together as you shop, choosing and counting three apples, three packets, four potatoes. Use words and gestures to reinforce concepts such as 'all gone,' 'again' and 'more'. Use a lively animated voice to sing, chant, whisper - an exaggerated gasp is often the best way to grab their attention.

Developmental Stage 3

Children (22-40 months)

Search for numbers and count together whenever you are out and about. Begin by counting stationary objects, but then move onto counting objects that are moving - cars, people getting on a bus and so on. Use number language such as 'more' and 'lots' to talk about familiar everyday object as you go out of the setting. Reinforce these experiences in the setting by bringing back a bundle of twigs from the park to stack, count and dig with.

Developmental Stages 4 & 5

Older children (40-60+ months)

Encourage older children to guess before counting the number of objects – such as the number of books in a pile at the library, or apples in a bag at the shop. Practice taking a glance and guessing, then counting how many items are in a group, such as ducks on a pond. Begin to record by using a simple tally system. Look at patterns and shapes in nature, leaves on a stem, spots on a ladybird. Use big number words – hundreds of leaves, thousands of bricks in a wall.

Developmental Stages 5 & 6

Bricks

Fabric or wooden bricks, stacking bricks, interlocking bricks and an endless array of construction toys offer wide opportunities for all aspects of problem solving, reasoning and numeracy as well as pretend play. Use bricks across the whole early years stage to develop babies' and children's early counting skills.

Young babies (0-11 months)

From around six months, babies will hold a soft brick placed in their hands and may bring it up to their face for a better look. From six months onwards babies may start to use two hands together, reaching for and grasping bricks and transferring small bricks from one hand to another. Collect a variety of different textured, soft, easily manipulated bricks for babies to explore with hands, feet and mouths.

Developmental Stage 1

Babies (8-20 months)

Build towers of soft bricks for babies to knock down. Take turns to place bricks on the stack, or offer the baby the last brick for the tower. Say 'One, Two, Three Go,' before knocking down the tower. Find bricks with bells or other small obejcts inside, or holes for little fingers to poke. Enjoy throwing soft bricks into a big box, taking turns and counting for the baby. Try dropping bricks in a noisy containerfor more counting fun.

Developmental Stage 2

Young children (16-26 months)

Easy interlocking bricks and magnetic blocks are perfect for very young children. Begin by helping children to pull bricks apart so they can rebuild them. At this stage the children will be happy to build towers but are not generally ready to use the bricks to make models of objects. You could create long lines of walls, bridges together, and use early mathematical language such as 'lots,' 'a few,' 'more,' 'same,' and position words such as 'in,' 'on' and 'under'.

Developmental Stage 3

Children (22-40 months)

Work together with the children to create patterns, bridges, steps, walls. Count how many bricks you needed. Encourage children to play co-operatively in small groups, staying near to support turn taking. Begin to introduce the words of comparison, 'taller,' 'shorter,' 'longer,' 'shorter,' 'few,' 'many'. Help the children to share out the bricks, one each in a box or basket for each child and then round again. Play a simple 'Snap' game with matching bricks.

Developmental Stages 4 & 5

Older children (40-60+ months)

Add blank sticky labels and pens, and printed number labels for children to count and label bricks and the structures they make. Use bricks in sand and water play or with dough or malleable materials. Play alongside, suggesting that children might guess or estimate how many bricks are used or needed. Compare towers and other structures, or use trucks or trains to carry bricks away in simple first subtraction, sharing or addition games.

Developmental Stages 5 & 6

Pretend Play

Pretend play involves babies and chidlren in exploring everyday objects, imitating what they see others do. Later, developing sequences and using objects symbolically, or playing with miniatures helps babies and young children to understand the purpose of counting, steadily becoming competent and confident in their counting skills.

Young babies (0-11 months)

Play Clap Hands or Peek-a-Boo and sing to babies to engage their attention. Pause in the middle of a game or song and wait for a vocalization asking you to continue. With older babies, use the language of possession as you play, sing and talk about what you are doing, such as teddy's hat, baby's hat, *name*'s shoes and so on. This understanding of possession is an important precursor to developing one-to-one correspondence.

Developmental Stage 1

Babies (8-20 months)

Offer a treasure basket of simple everyday objects such as a doll, flannel, brush, cup, spoon, hat and shoes. Make sure the objects are easy to manage for small hands and safe to be explored in the baby's mouth. Play alongside older babies, encouraging imitation of your simple pretend play, cuddling the doll, brushing hair and so on. Talk about and count body parts on the child, doll and yourself. 'Look two hands, one, two'.

Developmental Stage 2

Young children (16-26 months)

Try some simple tea set play, pouring and counting up to three cups of tea, putting pretend cakes on three plates, putting a spoon in each cup and so on. This will provide lots of opportunities for matching, sharing and pairing objects, one to one. At this stage the props need to look real but be safe to mouth. Try plastic fruit, clean safe food packaging and real plastic spoons. Or print and stick food pictures on paper plates for more first counting play.

Developmental Stage 3

Children (22-40 months)

By now, children's interest and focus for imaginative play is often around people they meet every day, such as shop play, postal workers, doctors, builders. Look for counting opportunities in every imaginative play set up, indoors and outside. Take a look at the home corner. Has it got a telephone with numbers, take away lists, calculators, TV remote controls, telephone directory, weighing scales, money, food items with prices marked, and a washing line?

Developmental Stages 4 & 5

Older children (40-60+ months)

Add opportunities for counting and recording numbers. Set up a simple café for lots of counting and order taking. Add number plates to bikes and push-alongs, create speed limit signs and do your own playground traffic survey. Use a train set or miniature cars for counting and sorting, setting up traffic jams, garages and stations. Encourage counting in twos, fives and tens, and estimating how many. Use words to describe position - 'first,' 'second,' 'third' and so on.

Developmental Stages 5 & 6

Games

At every point in the Early Years Foundation Stage, babies and young children will enoy playing games, taking turns, imitating, initiating activities and making choices, as they developing their early counting skills. Games should form part of every child's experience every day.

Young babies (0-11 months)

From birth, babies notice changes in the world around them. Focus their attention by providing a variety of bright, reflective, or black and white contrasting patterns for them to gaze at or touch. Offer babies objects and textures to pat and squeeze as well as identical objects to bang together - wooden bricks, small plastic bowls, plastic beakers or rattles. Practice clapping too - this is great preparation for counting games to come.

Developmental Stage 1

Babies (8-20 months)

Babies at this stage love games with an instant result, such as knocking down towers of bricks, stacking beakers, exploring activity centre toys, and hammering toys. Sing and count, whisper and count, clap and count as you play these games together. Use 'One, Two, Three' to build anticipation in the games and to introduce early mathematical language. Remember 'All gone' is perhaps the first step towards understanding the concept of nothing or zero.

Sitters, Standers and Explorers

Young children (16-26 months)

Play simple matching and sorting games, starting with matching real, everyday objects and then matching photographs and clear pictures of those objects. Children at this age love to fill and empty containers, so count together as they fill and empty buckets, boxes, bags and purses, and provide small bags and baskets for colecting. Build turn taking skills by encouraging them to take turns to place a brick on a tower, post a letter in a box, pull objects from a bag.

Developmental Stage 3

Children (22-40 months)

Around this time, children begin to enjoy simple board games such as picture lotto, picture and number dominoes and simple board games in groups of up to four children. Focus on developing one-to-one correspondence as each child counts. Remember to make the most of the Internet and CD ROM for some highly visual and interactive counting games. Plan counting games such as skittles, target games, and some parachute games for outside.

Developmental Stages 4 & 5

Older children (40-60+ months)

Look out for number games and songs that involve taking away, and adding more on. Play traditional games such as 'What's the Time Mr. Wolf?' for counting paces and estimating how many more. Use the language of comparing numbers, greater, less than in the games. Race small cars and use ordinal numbers, such as first, second, third. Use playground chalk to make simple games on the path or patio, and play with bean bags or quoits.

Developmental Stages 5 & 6

Posting and Stacking

Posting boxes and stacking toys rpovide practice in matching, sorting, ordering and comparing shapes - all important mathematical skills which complement early counting skills. Use posting and stacking play to practice counting and to build firm foundations in numeracy.

Young babies (0-11 months)

Young babies will pat, grasp and reach out for small shapes and rings. Look for easily manipulated soft rings for first reaching and grasping, solid objects are harder to grip and pass from hand to hand. Once babies can pass objects from one hand to another, encourage them to use two hands together to manipulate small objects and to bang two rings or other items together.

Developmental Stage 1

Babies (8-20 months)

At the beginning of this stage babies will enjoy grasping and dropping toys and will soon be able to release objects intentionally. Sing 'One, Two, Three, Go,' as babies drop objects into a tin or basket. Encourage older babies to post objects into a large hole cut into the top of a shoe box, or to push them into the top of a bag or basket. Ask 'more?' and comment 'All gone' as you play with them.

Developmental Stage 2

Young children (16-26 months)

Choose very simple shape sorting boxes, with only three shapes to be posted. Sound shape sorters reward the child with a squeak as the shape is matched to the hole. Watch how children use trial and error and later visually match the shape to the hole before posting. For the youngest children, post balls, cars, and small everyday objects down cardboard tubes. Try ring stacking toys where rings are put on a simple rod or large plastic bangles put over a plastic beaker.

Developmental Stage 3

Children (22-40 months)

As children's visual discrimination skills develop, shape sorters can be more complex, with shapes to be posted into the holes at a particular angle. Count the shapes together before they go into the box, and again as they are all tipped out. Use a lively animated singing voice or perhaps try whispering to gain and hold the child's attention. Sort and count rings for stacking. Talk about which ring goes on first, second, third and so on.

Developmental Stages 4 & 5

Older children (40-60+ months)

Older children will enjoy nesting toys, such as Billy's Barrels or Russian Dolls. Hide different quantities of sequins or small buttons in each nest and estimate and then count how many. Tip all the buttons out and find our how many altogether. Engage the most active children in running, jumping and counting games out of doors, taking their whole bodies through tubes and boxes. Use counting as a timer. Begin to use a simple tally method to record counts and scores.

Developmental Stages 5 & 6

Paint, Paper and Scissors

All babies and young children can enjoy paint and paper and use this activity to develop counting skills and understanding of number. From tearing and daubing to creating intricate counted patterns, there are endless opportunities from birth to the end of the Foundation Stage.

Young babies (0-11 months)

Sing to young babies, clapping and splashing in soapy water, using baby shampoo to make the bubbles safe for young eyes. Try exploring whipped mashed potato, or whipped cream for some messy play, patting, smearing and squeezing with fingers and fists. Use words and signs or gestures for 'Again,' 'More,' and 'All gone' – which will help the earliest understanding of number and counting language.

Developmental Stage 1

Babies (8-20 months)

At this stage, babies enjoy exploring paint and paper. Try tearing long strips of paper and rolling paper into balls. Count one two three and then rip the paper or throw it into a big box. Count daubs as the children paint. Use simple objects or sponges for printing, counting 'One, Two, Three' as each mark is made. Paint finger tips, counting as you go, before babies try a little finger painting. Try it with toes too for a messier session – best outside or in an empty paddling pool.

Developmental Stage 2

Young children (16-26 months)

Tear pictures from old magazines to stick, counting as you go, or count as you tear lon strips of paper. Body parts are a great way to introduce counting to such young children, two eyes, two ears, one nose, ten toes and so on. Try poking fingers through tissue paper and counting them, put tiny dabs of paint on fingers and toes and count as you go. Sing and talk about two eyes, two ears and one nose. Make finger prints and holes in foam, paint and dough.

Developmental Stage 3

Children (22-40 months)

Paint patterns and shapes on huge pieces of paper and then try tiny pictures with cotton buds on tiny slips of paper, counting to five and back again as you paint tiny objects. Try snipping with scissors and counting together as you go. Start to create simple repeated patterns, stripes and so on. Work with groups of children to create props for number rhymes and songs, such as Ten Green Bottles, or Five Currant Buns in the Bakers Shop.

Developmental Stages 4 & 5

Older children (40-60+ months)

Paint alongside children, creating and counting groups of objects, such as five fishes, ten cats and so on. Use these for simple counting games. Paint your own spotty dominoes and cut them out for a giant game. Create paint or collage number lines for talking about one more, one less and so on. Paint pairs of creatures for a Noah's ark theme and practise counting in twos, using a washing line and some pegs to matching cut out pictures in pairs.

Developmental Stages 5 & 6

Food

Mealtimes and snack time, as well as cooking and baking activities offer wonderful opportunities to count, share, talk about and compare quantities, as well as to use the language of counting, including 'all gone,' 'more,' 'less,' 'same' or 'equal'.

The one-to-one focus of mealtimes is a good opportunity to sing and play with young babies. Grab the baby's attention by calling their name and using an exaggerated gasp, then sing first counting and finger rhymes such as 'Round and Round the Garden Like a Teddy Bear,' 'Two Little Dickey Birds,' or 'This Little Piggy'. Clapping games are also fun at this intimate time.

Developmental Stage 1

At this stage, babies love to explore food and become gradually more independent. Offer real choices, such as 'Would you like one sandwich or two?' and 'Would you like more', and say, sign or gesture 'All gone'. Try simple food related activities, such as breaking up bread to feed ducks, count as each bit is pulled off the slice and placed in the bag, squeeze and pull off lumps of bread dough, spoon jelly from one container to another, count spoonfuls.

Developmental Stage 2

Young children (16-26 months)

Simple, no cook food preparation offers lots of opportunities for stirring, rolling, tearing, whipping food and so on. Try stirring sugar or flour into water, rolling pastry and dough, whipping cream, crumbling sponges and so on. Use first number words as you count to five. Focus on building children's understanding of possession, *name*'s spoon, my spoon, as well as beginning to build one-to-one correspondence with objects and food items.

Developmental Stage 3

Children (22-40 months)

Baking now offers real possibilities for counting. Count spoonfuls, count equipment, look at the numbers on the scales, measuring jug and measuring spoons. Make a plate of biscuits or a pizza to share, as well as dips that can be spooned out to be shared. Try fruity kebabs on straws for counting and making patterns, or smoothies and fruit salads, mixing three grapes, two spoonfuls of yoghurt and one piece of banana, using different measures.

Developmental Stages 4 & 5

Older children (40-60+ months)

Encourage independence as older children prepare food following picture recipes and counting out ingredients. Help them to record quantities of ingredients, using pictures, drawings, marks or a tally system. Prepare segmented fruit together, talking about numbers of segments. Make food for real occasions. Help the children to estimate how many apple slices will be needed for snack time, or sandwiches for a picnic.

Developmental Stages 5 & 6

Get Active!

Physical play is important for babies' and children's development, health and emotional well-being. Babies and young children learn through doing, so active play is a perfect way for children to experience counting in a lively, enjoyable and energetic way.

Young babies (0-11 months)

Dance with young babies, enjoying the shared experience, keeping a steady beat in the music or a song, and pausing often to give the baby opportunities to indicate they want more. Rock babies gently in a blanket and then ask 'More?' Give older babies plenty of opportunities for rolling and wriggling. Provide different materials and textures for the child to sit, roll, wriggle and crawl on.

Developmental Stage 1

Babies (8-20 months)

At this stage, babies need to use their increasing mobility to discover the world. Sing rhymes for bouncing and jigging – there are plenty of traditional rhymes to choose from in books and on the internet. Roll large beach balls through tunnels and down gentle slopes for the baby to follow and explore. Count 'One, Two, Three, Go,' before rolling toys to the baby. Count as you carry them up steps and round your setting.

Developmental Stage 2

Young children (16-26 months)

Encourage imitative and 'Follow the Leader' type play, such as 'Everybody Do This, Everybody Do This, Just Like Me'. Try three stamps, three claps. Count together as you place three balls in a bucket and then enjoy tossing them in the air. Play ring games that introduce counting to three, such as 'Ring-a-Ring-a-Roses' or try dancing together to music and then 'One, two, three, we all fall down.' as you collapse together on the floor.

Developmental Stage 3

Children (22-40 months)

At this age children love treasure hunts. Hide lots of red, green and blue bricks and ask children to find three bricks, or five red bricks. Children with a good understanding of counting could look for two red bricks <u>and</u> two green bricks etc. Another time, ask the children to gather natural materials such as twigs or leaves, then count each collection and talk about most, fewest. Wheelbarrows, shopping trolleys and pushchairs are ideal for collecting.

Developmental Stages 4 & 5

Older children (40-60+ months)

Try lots of simple race games or obstacle courses, with plenty of opportunities for first, second, third, as well as counting up to ten and more, or back from zero. Chalk a number line outside to practice counting in twos, counting one more, finding one less. There are lots of singing and dancing games for counting back from ten, such as 'Ten Green Bottles,' 'Five Little Speckled Frogs'. Get a copy of **This Little Puffin** for lots more ideas.

Developmental Stages 5 & 6

Songs, Stories and Rhymes

There is a wealth of excellent picture books for counting and talking about number. They often combine rhythm and rhyme with visually appealing illustrations to capture babies' and young children's attention. Combine these books with follow-on activities to reinforce the counting and language used.

Young babies (0-11 months)

Remember that very young babies focus best at 15 to 25 centimetres at eye level. Look for books with black and white patterns to encourage looking, as well as soft rag books and photo books. Try **Faces** by John Fordham, Macmillan, a black and white rag book. Mealtimes, washing and dressing times are ideal opportunities for some simple 'One two three' finger rhyme play. Old favourites are usually the best, or talk to parents to find out what their babies enjoy.

Developmental Stage 1

Babies (8-20 months)

At this stage babies need to share books one-to-one or perhaps with one other older baby. Look for counting books with textures, holes for little fingers to poke through, such as **The Hungry Caterpillar** by Eric Carle, Picture Puffin, **Ten Little Monkeys Jumping on the Bed** by Tina Freeman, Child's Play, or books with small flaps to lift such as **Baby Animals** by John Butler, Usborne. Keep sessions short with lots of finger play, clapping, counting and singing too.

Developmental Stage 2

Young children (16-26 months)

Use props to make counting books and rhymes more real for young children. You only need one or two very simple props to really engage the attention of children. Remember too, that at this stage children thrive on the familiar, with frequent repetition. Offer choice of number rhymes and stories, allowing children to make their choice with a glance, a point, a reach or with words. As you plan a theme or topic, include counting rhymes and books that will reinforce learning.

Developmental Stage 3

Children (22-40 months)

'Emeka's Gift' by Ifeoma Onyefulu, Francis Lincoln Books, is an African counting book with engaging photographs, offering lots of opportunity for counting as well as talking about other families and cultures. For a very different counting adventure find 'My Granny Went to Market' by Stella Blackstone, Barefoot Books. At this stage children are beginning to enjoy small group play, so try some dancing in a ring games, such as The Hokey Cokey.

Developmental Stages 4 & 5

der children (40-60+ months)

Now children are ready to practise counting in pairs, and later in fives and tens, as well as starting to combine two groups of objects as addition and a first understanding of subtraction or taking away. Count pairs of hands or feet for counting in twos, and for fives and tens fingers or toes. Look out for story books, songs and rhymes for counting back from ten, such as 'Five Little Men in a Flying Saucer' or 'Ten Fat Sausages'. Or try www.tttools.com/assets/images/COUNTING_BY_2s.

Developmental Stages 5 & 6

Matching and Sorting

Finding the same, sorting, spotting differences, comparing and ordering are all essential in developing numeracy. Matching and sorting play helps children see how they can make sense of a jumble of objects and rearrange them, clarifying understanding of early concepts essential to counting and early numeracy.

Young babies (0-11 months)

Even very young babies can notice changes in groupings of object. Babies need lots of opportunity to explore everyday objects and look at photographs of everyday objects. Create a treasure basket of matching objects, such as two bricks, two rattles, two socks, two brushes and so on. Try putting a sock on each hand and encourage the baby to bring these together to explore. Use the baby's name first and say '*Name*, look, same.'

Developmental Stage 1

Babies (8-20 months)

Try matching objects to photographs of the object, starting with the child's own possessions, such as their hat or shoes. As well as learning about matching and first counting, children also learn about possession, my shoes, mummy's hat and so on. Understanding of possession is a first step towards one-to-one correspondence. Encourage babies to select objects from a choice of two by stretching out your hand and asking the baby to give you the spoon.

Developmental Stage 2

Young children (16-26 months)

At this stage children love to help with everyday chores, and this is a great opportunity for counting, sorting and finding the same. Try washing and drying dishes from the home corner together. Match the pots and pans, sort the cups and saucers, and put a spoon in each cup. Chores outside such as washing the outdoor toys together, offer endless opportunities for finding the same, counting wheels, sorting types and colours.

Developmental Stage 3

Children (22-40 months)

Matching an object to another identical object, object to photograph, object to line drawing, line drawing to line drawing - the many different types of matching to be mastered at this stage, but all offer opportunities for use the language of counting and practicing counting itself. Each time, count how many in each group. Hide buttons, small animals or counters for sorting in sand or water tray, or natural materials outside, such as a pile of leaves or twigs.

Developmental Stages 4 & 5

Older children (40-60+ months)

Pretend money, coins and notes are fascinating for children of this age. Make piles of ten coins and practise counting in ten. Do lots of sharing out of money or cards, one for you, one for you and so on, or perhaps five for you, five for you. Count and sort objects by more than one factor, such as size and colour. Help the children to use counting and sorting for a real purpose, such as counting and sorting seeds before planting, or who wants milk or juice.

Developmental Stages 5 & 6

33

Dough and More

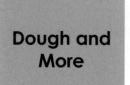

Messy play with interesting textures and smells, and different properties offers excellent opportunity for babies and children to explore the concepts on which the foundations of mathematics are built. For older children, dough play offers real opportunities to use their counting skills for a clear purpose.

Young babies (0-11 months)

Offer cooked and cooled bowls of egg noodles for safe play. The noodles are great for older babies trying to grasp with finger and thumbs, and are easy to pick up with a palmer grasp. The noodles can be trailed through the fingers of younger babies and are great for squeezing and patting. Try tickling the palm of the babies hand with a noodle as you sing 'Round and Round the Garden'.

Developmental Stage 1

Babies (8-20 months)

Use a pizza or bread dough, or a simple flour and water dough. Encourage babies to pinch of lumps of dough, perhaps placing each one in a small cup or section of an ice cube tray. This is great for one-to-one correspondence. Also, roll out the dough and cut rounds. Encourage the baby to add a plastic shape or some dried pasta to each round as another one-to-one activity.

Developmental Stage 2

Young children (16-26 months)

Add plastic plates to the dough play and help the children to create plates of pretend dough food, one sausage, two eggs and so on. Create a dough birthday cake and add plastic straws as candles - how many candles should we have, one or two? Try spooning gloop (cornflour and water) into small trays, such as a sorting tray. Sing as you spoon or stir. 'This is the way we stir the mix, stir the mix, stir the mix, this is the way we stir the mix one, two, three.'

Developmental Stage 3

Children (22-40 months)

Children will love to make their own dough mixtures, experimenting with different recipes, working alongside other children, counting spoonfuls and measuring the liquids in cups. Encourage children to guess how many spoonfuls or cups they would need to fill the bowl. Count together, sometimes, pausing to see if the children continue counting alone. Practise sharing out the dough, 'One for you, one for you', or 'One for you, one for me'.

Developmental Stages 4 & 5

Older children (40-60+ months)

At this stage, children can try and follow a simple pictorial recipe with minimum adult assistance, and encourage them to experiment with their dough making. Try some hardening dough to create objects for themed number lines, ideal for counting practice. Make food, sea life or dinosaur shapes. Use these shapes to play a shop game, with coins, for practice in counting, adding and taking away. Try asking questions such as 'Have you got enough to give me three?'

Developmental Stages 5 & 6

Cars, Diggers and Trains

From simply rolling cars back and forth, to creating complex roadways or counting train carriages. Small car and train play is an excellent way to use mathematical language and to begin counting. It is ideal for children who enjoy solitary play but can be easily extended to small group games.

Young babies (0-11 months)

Look out for easy to grasp small cars, safe for mouths. Try some simple 'Ready, steady, go' play, as you roll the car towards the baby. Look for noisy bright cars and trains that are easy for the baby to track as they move. Pull along trains are ideal for discovering cause and effect - as I pull this string, the train comes. Look out for cars that you press down and they move gently away. Encourage older babies to bang two vehicles together.

Developmental Stage 1

Babies (8-20 months)

Take turns with babies to release cars and trains down a gentle slope, saying 'One, two, three, GO!'. Encourage older babies to add carriages to simple chunky easy to handle trains. Count the carriages. Practise lining up and counting trains and cars, counting every time. Create little sheds or garages from small boxes, with one shed for every train or car for one-to-one correspondence as they drive the vehicles in.

Developmental Stage 2

Young children (16-26 months)

Gather a bucketful of cars and trains for sorting and counting. Add some tunnels or bridges for creating traffic jams. Play alongside the children, providing a simple commentary, with an emphasis on mathematical language and counting at every opportunity. Encourage counting and sorting, but don't become too obsessed with your agenda - listen to what the children are thinking and working on! Match or sort cars, arrange in pairs or groups of three.

Developmental Stage 3

Children (22-40 months)

At this stage children enjoy pretend play, so why not create a train from large cardboard boxes and number each carriage. Children can load soft toys into each carriage, counting as they go, or perhaps add pretend freight, using old cereal cartons and similar boxes. How many will fit in each carriage? Have fun with trains and tracks, finding out how many trains will fit on the bridge, how many carriages each engine can pull.

Developmental Stages 4 & 5

Older children (40-60+ months)

At this stage, children can start to record their counting using a simple tally system, or counters. Try some digger play, estimating how many scoops of sand the digger will need to fill a box. Offer sticky labels to add numbers to small cars on a race track or to carriages and trains, then put the cars in order. This book will focus attention as older children can explore some bigger numbers with a train theme, **Long train – 101 Cars on the Track**, Ken Wilson-Max, Cartwheel.

Developmental Stages 5 & 6

Make it Happen

From activity centres to battery operated and switched toys, photocopiers, digital cameras, printers and the computer, there is an endless array of resources that can be used to enable babies and children to discover how they can use everyday technology to explore their world and at the same time move towards being confident in counting.

Young babies (0-11 months)

Toys with flaps, buttons, bells, holes for fingers to investigate, and activity centres all offer babies an opportunity to explore and discover the effect their actions can have on objects. Count babies in to actions with a 'One, Two Three, Pull!'. Play lots of clapping and patting games, counting and singing as you go.

Developmental Stage 1

Babies (8-20 months)

Older babies will enjoy operating simple switch or battery operated toys, pressing a switch, or pulling a lever to make things happen. At this stage babies love to explore an object hidden inside another. Tuck rattles inside socks, bells inside gloves and so on. Provide lots of opportunities for hammering and banging and sing the familiar song 'Peter Hammers with One Hammer all Day Long'. Create a treasure basket of things that come apart, Velcro, magnetic blocks etc.

Developmental Stage 2

Young children (16-26 months)

At this stage children are fascinated with buttons and dials, so toy telephones for babbling and first words are ideal. Play alongside young children using simple mathematical language, such as 'more,' 'again,' 'all gone,' and counting 'one two three' at every opportunity. Opening and shutting boxes and bags with easy fasteners will fascinate at this age, as well as emptying and filling containers. Collect lots of small bags and boxes and put one small toy animal or brick in each.

Developmental Stage 3

Children (22-40 months)

Simple computer programs offer plenty of opportunities for use of the space bar to produce actions and, for older children, simple counting activities. Choose programs where you can control the level, so children can start counting stationary objects with plenty of time to respond. moving on to moving objects, working against the clock and using mouse skills such as 'drag and drop' to make choices. Match the program level to individuals.

Developmental Stages 4 & 5

Older children (40-60+ months)

As well as CDROM and web based counting games, older children can practise their counting skills and put them to practical use. Try activities involving use of a photocopier, digital camera, overhead projector or interactive whiteboard. Look for programs that extend their skills, not just in terms of being able to count a greater number of objects, but also counting in twos, fives, or tens, counting objects that can't be seen, estimating how many objects may be needed.

Developmental Stages 5 & 6

Existing and planned titles in the Baby and Beyond series include:

* Messy Play
* The Sensory World
* Sound and Music
* The Natural World
* Construction
* Mark Making
* Dolls and Soft Toys
* Bikes, Prams & Pushchairs
* Finger Play and Rhymes

* Role Play
* Food and Cooking
* Dens, Shelters & Play Outside
* Small World Play
* Counting
* Tell Me a Story (2009)
* Movement and Beat (2009)
* Going Out (2009)
* About Me! (2009)